SINGING *Over* BONES

SINGING *Over* BONES

Poems of Love and Resistance

AMY SINGH

Om Books International

First published in 2025 by

Om Books International

Corporate & Editorial Office
A-12, Sector 64, Noida 201 301
Uttar Pradesh, India
Phone: +91 120 477 4100
Email: editorial@ombooks.com
Website: www.ombooksinternational.com

Sales Office
107, Ansari Road, Darya Ganj,
New Delhi 110 002, India
Phone: +91 11 4000 9000
Email: sales@ombooks.com
Website: www.ombooks.com

Copyright © Amy Singh 2025

ALL RIGHTS RESERVED. No part of this book may be reproduced or transmitted in any form by any means, electronic or mechanical, including photocopying and recording, or by any information storage and retrieval system, except as may be expressly permitted in writing by the publisher.

ISBN: 978-93-6395-576-9

Printed in India

10 9 8 7 6 5 4 3 2 1

For Harbans and Gurcharan—

*My grandmothers,
keepers of stories, riddles, poetry, and hugs.
The very essence of love and resilience.*

whatever returns from oblivion, returns to find a voice.

– Louise Glück

Contents

Introduction   *xiii*

Static

In Which Prayer Exhausts Itself into Poetry	3
What Would You Like to Eat?	4
Fatigue	5
In Our Home	6
Watchdog	7
Inside Out	8
Leave Application that Never Left My Outbox	10
Vanishing Act	11
Anniversary Dinner	12
This Farewell Was Once a Love Song	13

Folk

Genesis	17
Relic	18
Khan Baba	19

Veil	22
The Wrong Door	23
Found Poetry	24
Evidence	25
Ancestors	26
Achilles Heel	27
Ropar	29
I Am Not My Name	30
Hisaab (Hindi)	31
Sunflowers	34
Daarji	36
Daughters of Sky	37
Water under the Flame	39
I Was in Several People's Dreams Last Night	40
In Case of Emergency	42

Requiems and Laments

To the One Who Asked Me, 'Shall I Book a Cab for You?'	47
Broken People	48
Antinome	49
In Which I Confess and Curse	50
Agar Magar (Hindi)	52
Is This What Dying Feels Like?	53
Held Captive	54
Dil Kya Hai (Hindi)	55
In Which I Ask for Towels	56
Broken Antenna	57
The Descent	58
After the Flood	59

Yaani (Hindi)	60
The Body Keeps a Score	62
Kal Shaam (Hindi)	63
Drowning	64

Protest Pop

Aftermath	67
Shehar (Panjabi)	69
Barish (Hindi)	70
Yeh Kavita Ek Elaan Hai (Hindi)	74
Hathkadiyan (Hindi)	78
Agar Ab Bhi Chup Rahe (Hindi)	79
Sar-e-aam (Hindi)	83
Naakaar (Hindi)	84
Letter to Lahore: Are You Cold Too?	85
Pyaare Lahore (Panjabi)	87
Letter to Lahore: Friendship Day	89
Letter to Lahore: Daak	91

Soft Rock and Serenades

Tonight	97
Note to Self	98
Love Thy Enemy	99
Faustian Bargain	100
Too Many	101
Tweezer	102
A Wall	104
Camouflage	106
This Too Is a Prayer	107

Vessel	108
Shards of Truth	109
Arrival	110
Kavita Da Safar (Panjabi)	111
Mad Woman	115
Mahila Munch	116
Cheesecake	118
In Which I Rescue Beauty	119
Calvary	121
Autumn's Hope	122
Khud Farebi (Hindi)	123
Are You Still in Love with Me?	125
Balm	126
One Thing	127
Two Pigeons	129
Surma (Panjabi)	131
What Should I Call You?	132
Salvage	133
To-do List of Love	134
Two Tunes	135
Naghma (Hindi)	136
In the Language of Trees	138
Love, Like Laundry	140
What Is, Is	141
Ghar (Panjabi)	142
Answered Prayers	144
Plato Said Poets Are Liars— Then Why Do They Live Forever?	145
Acknowledgements	148

Introduction

Marble feels warm beneath my tiny feet. Sunlight falls across the arches and jharokhas of Jal Mahal in Pinjore Gardens. People gather around an old man, his back resting against a wooden door that opens to nowhere. His clothes are ragged, his hair untamed. He plays the flute, and only then breaks mid-tune into poetry.

Everyone calls him Khan Baba. He smiles at my mother with sad, knowing eyes.

This is a scene from my childhood. This is the story of Khan Baba. When his wife abandoned him in Pinjore Gardens, he could never leave this place. It became his sanctuary and a shrine for his longing. Even between eight and ten years old, when I remember meeting him several times, I sensed that he was sad. But it wasn't the downtrodden kind of sadness that begged for pity. His sorrow felt like a hammer striking destiny's walls—the kind that carves tunnels to freedom.

A similar sadness lived in my mother. She didn't look sad, and perhaps she couldn't. She was a single mother with three children in a world that traded strength for survival. Where was the space to grieve? Most days, she cloaked her sadness behind practicality. But when she sat next to Khan Baba, something shifted. Her broken parts, usually hidden, found air.

For my siblings and me, those days in the gardens felt like picnics. For her, they were something sacred: brief moments of reprieve.

I didn't know then that grief could be inherited, like blood—flowing through generations. I could sense the shape of something I couldn't yet articulate. But like my mother, like Khan Baba, I had already begun to write poetry.

In the early noughties, Khan Baba died of cancer. In 2008, cancer took my mother too. Grief within their bones ultimately devoured them both.

This terrified me. If pain was the riverbed of poetry, its birthplace, I sensed I was fertile for it by design. Having lost one parent to death and the other to life, I feared that grief would drown me if I didn't pour it out.

By the time I was twenty-eight, I had lost four grandparents, my mother, my mamu, and my massi. Death came so often it became a choking hazard. I turned to paper like one turns to God. Not for the sake of poetry, but for self-preservation.

Through writing, I met myself. I unlayered my identity: ancestral, colonial, cultural, and lingual. I searched for meaning, for hope. Rilke reminded me that no feeling is final. So I moved between languages—Panjabi, Hindustani, English—each carrying its own truth. I moved from poet to poet looking for resonance. Shiv Kumar Batalvi and Shah Hussain's sublime Birha. Faiz and Pash's revolutionary fire. Amrita Pritam and Parveen Shakir's fierce tenderness. They showed me that poetry, like love, transcends mere catharsis.

It becomes whatever we need it to be: shelter, weapon, balm, or wings.

Over time, my pain began to mirror the fractures around me. As my country entered a majoritarian age, old wounds were reopened for political gain. Violence broke out in universities like PU, DU, and JNU. Students, like Gurmehar Kaur, faced threats for speaking up. We saw divisiveness creep into public spaces. That's when Sabika Abbas Naqvi and I took our poetry there too.

I found belonging there—poetry in streets and parks, free from hierarchies of stage and status. These gatherings weren't institutional or commercial; they were communion. They opened doors to storytelling and listening that couldn't be otherwise unlocked.

During this time, I was also repairing my inner self. I read *Women Who Run with the Wolves* by Dr Clarissa Pinkola Estés. In this book, she talks about La Loba, the mythic, folkloric wolf woman, who gathers the bones of wolves. When she has gathered the entire skeleton, she raises her arms and begins to sing. As she sings, the bones flesh out and become furred. She sings until the wolf breathes, until it runs into the canyons. The metaphor spoke to me deeply. It awakened a La Loba within me—a bone-gatherer searching for fragments of my life, my lineage, my loss. From the darkest places, I retrieved pieces of myself and began to sing them back to life.

Living became a process of creative repair. Singing Over Bones, more than a title—it became ritual, invocation, and prayer.

You hold in your hands a decade-long process of excavation and resurrection.

In *Static*, I explore the disorientation of losing myself and my place in the world. Trying to find clarity after surviving an abusive partnership, concussion and PTSD. *Folk* reaches back to the familial and ancestral, asking who I am and where I come from. *Requiems and Laments* invites grief to the forefront, revelling in its brutal honesty. *Protest Pop* braids the personal and political, transforming private pain into collective resistance. And *Soft Rock and Serenades* guards my tender heart, like a dragon protecting its hoard.

Over the past ten years of writing and performing, I've come to see that grief or love is not just personal. It is often generational, communal—a thread binding us through time and space. These poems are my offering: to resist, to forgive, to love, and to belong.

Much like Khan Baba of Pinjore Gardens, I invite you to gather here—in this marble porch of vulnerability. Where you may find your own bones, your own song, your own La Loba. Where the doors that seem to open to nowhere might lead us back to ourselves or to each other.

STATIC

In Which Prayer Exhausts Itself into Poetry

My love is washing dishes (or blood from his hands)
I am lying down, in the wake of the ritual.

Our bed is his altar of burnt offerings
and battered flesh,
He, Adam;
I, the lamb.

We go to the same church but his God
doesn't answer my calls.

What Would You Like to Eat?

I no longer know   *like*

I have fed on your lies for so long,
truth tastes funny in my mouth.

I was your beloved once,
now wedded to your side chicks   *whores*

I was a person once, now I am an idea
  yours

I was in love once, now I am ____
  lost

(nothing I want is on the menu)
I was a woman once. Now I am a Ghost.

They don't eat.

Fatigue

He lets me
walk out
of the door
with hooks
inside my
ribcage.

    I labour.
    I shop.
    I laugh.

Sometimes, I meet
people—call them friends.
if I'm gone too long,
he simply tugs at the leash;
and I'm back to the kennel.

I missed you, he says.

    I look for a place close enough;
    for the ropes to loosen up
    and the hooks to comes off
    and my bones to catch a break
    from breaking tonight.

I missed you too, I say. I even smile.

In Our Home

things often
        b r e a k

vase from the side table
morning after dinner plates
my mother's jewellery
vermillion vows

I pick up
the wreckage after you

but
      I leave
my
           own
      pieces
                on
  the
        floor

Watchdog

Anger—your red rabid dog
has followed me into fear

in the day, I turn invisible
tiptoeing under its belly

in the night, no one's awake
there's nowhere to hide

Our house has two exit doors:
Death and Dream—opening
into each other

it guards them both, I rise
with teeth marks on my thighs.

Inside Out

Loving you
Is like tending to a monster inside you:
Walking with my head down,
Making no sound,
Breathing softly enough
To not wake you.

Loving you is like
Looking out of a window,
Keeping you as close as desire
Yet placing glass in-between,
Safely revealing myself to you.

But safety is an illusion here—
glass shatters under fists,
and the clock is a countdown
to your next explosion.

One misstep and you'll be up—
and when you break the glass,
who am I loving?
who am I becoming?
what happens on the inside
when there is no outside anymore?

Loving you is like holding a grenade with gardening mitts on my hands.

Leave Application that Never Left My Outbox

Last night, I slept on the floor, like a human doormat. Her feet pressing on my belly as she reached for his mouth. His heel choking my throat, as he took her lips, her laughter, her lingerie—hungry, thoughtless. This was my home—I planted trees here. Now I'm almost buried in the backyard.

They always come, these shiny strangers, slithering into our bed. This is always how my story ends.

As I write this, she's gone. And my love wants this doormat to be his magic carpet again.
I don't know if this will save us. How will he remove her from his lips before kissing me?

But I, the bitch-goddess of desperation, will spread my legs to feel something, anything. Because sometimes, his touch is the only proof I exist.

What curse, what choice, what destiny is this? I have to be a magic carpet in my marriage today, so I cannot be a manager at work.

I need a leave of sickness—until I find some self-respect and leave for good.

Vanishing Act

My lover has a way
of vaporising from the bedsheet,
from the soft pit of my belly button—graveyard of his seed.

He leaves the utterly unreliable
memory foam of my body
like fragrance leaves anniversary lilies.

He vanishes from the name plates,
and from speed dial—
love's withdrawal symptom.

He's got other woman
to wed;
in my stead.

Anniversary Dinner

By the pool, I watch you divide yourself. Like a cell splits: cleanly, without remorse.

Other women dance with the other you.

At home, you turn away. Like gods abandon mortals: slowly, then all at once.

How do I leave here?

I understand now how Persephone* felt, swallowing those seeds—each betrayal a pomegranate pearl, bitter and bright on the tongue.

Love is why I ate, and why I should spit.

---

* In Greek mythology, daughter of Zeus and Demeter, who became Queen of the Underworld after her abduction by Hades. Pomegranate seeds, which she was tricked into eating, bound her to the Underworld, as consuming food there obligated her to return.

This Farewell Was Once a Love Song

Our hands touched—
a throbbing vein on your
mount of Venus, tapped on
my fate's forked lines.

I imagined your wings
and you clipped mine.

Our song—
lovesick metaphor,
now pared down to the bone,
crashing against your heart of stone.

goodbye
goodbye
goodbye
old lover!

Our luck, it seems,
               is overdrawn.
I must leave. You are already
                           gone.

FOLK

Genesis

We all begin somewhere—
In the dutiful consummation
of something arranged,
In heat of moments
played on life's backstage,
In prophecy's promise
or curse's cage.
But some of us begin
in that sacred space
where two people
become gods in love.

Relic

My face—my father and mother's maiden art project,
abandoned mid-stroke, now it is time's adopted kid.
A genetical work in progress; fine poetry
written in the recesses of dark circles.
Secrets concealed by stubborn cheekbones
let slip by my landslide nose. One eye
full of curiosity, the other of trauma.
Eyebrows arching over beauty and terror.
Love clenched between crooked teeth,
fluttering to come out,
but my lips drip only honey, never the truth.
Oh, I can sweet-talk all you want, but
this artwork isn't meant for home decorations;
it's an artefact in the making,
an archaeological piece of evidence:
Some love lost, some love found.
Today, it bites the dust and smokes cigarettes
rolled from the letters of ex-lovers.
My face—a relic perfected in pain—
and left in vain.

Khan Baba

Year 1999: I am a seven-year-old girl
With ancient eyes and curious hands.
I want to understand everything my fingers touch,
To know everything my gaze falls upon.
We're out on a picnic at Pinjore Gardens,
And there ... my eyes fell on him.

To my seven-year-old self, he looked terrifying:
A shirt with black lungi,
White untamed hair cascading
like waterfalls over his shoulders.
I just wanted to disappear
Under the hem of my mother's firozi suit.
But before I could,
He looked at my sister, who must have been four,
And said:
'Kisi ki bazm mein guzre hue ae haseen lamhe,
Aa ke jee bhar ke tujhe pyaar karoon.*

That was the first sucker punch
of a memory-hole in my heart.

With my ancient eyes and curious hands, I learned:

---

* Those beautiful moments spent in someone's company, Come, let me love you to my heart's content.

Khan Baba had no home, no food to eat,
No family to call his own.
He never accepted alms,
But wrote poetry on crumpled papers,
Feeding on words as if his life depended on them.

Khan Baba smoked cigarettes, too many,
One after another, as if measuring time
Not by the hands of a clock,
But by the length of those burning sticks.

Now you can do the maths: how many cigarettes
it took to wait for the love of his life
In the same garden, for over thirty years?

His love never returned.
Perhaps he woke with ashes
in his mouth every morning. Or poetry.

Khan Baba carried so much sorrow and agony inside,
But never gave an ounce, a drop of his sadness to anyone else.

Instead, he took in others' sadness
and offered them temporary peace
At the cost of his constant pain.

Khan Baba died alone.

In my dreams, he speaks still:
Chala ja o raahi, chala ja o raahi…
Mujhe dekhne de khud apni tabahi…*

But I remain tethered to this spot,
where a seven-year-old girl once learned
that love can be a lifelong vigil.
—a deathless hope.

---

* Go away, oh traveller, go away, let me witness my own destruction.

Veil

Long before
I could know
my body
there was always a woman
who would hand me down a veil
to cover some parts of it.

There was
always a man
who tore into that veil
claiming his territory over
my organs.

The Wrong Door

In the hospital,
a girl searches for extra blankets,
for warmth. Opens a door.
Finds instead cold hands
that will never leave her.
A touch that is hard on her
soft growing body parts.

Eleven: the age at which
the world reveals its teeth.

Mother, too ill to ward shadows away,
Father only a name on admission forms.

Time passes. The girl grows,
forever searching for safety
in places that no longer exist.

Helpful hands, unmasked,
reach across years.

Their shadows fall
on every door she opens.

Found Poetry

Bus tickets take you places,
Like yesterday, I found an old one,
In my father's discarded wallet,
Worn leather exhaling musty years,
Ticket smudged, edges frayed.
A poem was scribbled on its back,
The bus went to Chandigarh,
Where did my father go?

Evidence

  Today
I ran
  my fingers
down
  my mother's
old ECG reports
  tracing the coloured lines ebbing
and arching
  against
a crisp sheet yellowed
  by time's dye, some lines dipping
lower than usual, some lifting higher
  than others, which
could sum up
  her
short bright existence—
  proof of a Life outlasting the life and
then I felt it:
HER HEART BEAT
fifteen years
  after it stopped, I felt it beating
on my fingertips. I don't know
  What to make of this.
here lies
  her evidence
but
  WHERE IS MY MOTHER?

Ancestors

I seek them in old recipes,
They hide in unpaid bills.

I seek them in distant relatives,
They hide in the mirror, still.

I seek them in tarot card readings,
They hide in memory's landfill.

I seek them in the pursuit of wisdom,
They hide in unforgiven sins.

I seek them in my unborn children,
They hide in abortion pills.

Achilles Heel

We are both made of pain—
my father and I.
If he hurts me,
he hurts himself, and the guilt
gets collected in the potholes
of the broken road we have travelled.
If I hurt him, it's not without scarring myself
with knives of history I never mean to repeat.

Our love is either lost in translation,
or the sun never shines in our silence-stuffed mouths.
The abruptness between our words has lasted
longer than the Trojan War.
If I had a horse made of a language
he could understand,
I would bleed my heart in its belly
and give it up as a truce.
But our egos are unconquered like Achilles,
with a misplaced heel.

If we weren't so similar,
We could have been closer.

I sit in front of a healer,
she tells me: *"these slips, trips and falls*

*are caused by bottled-up aggression
you have for yourself."*

How do I tell her?
It is because I know:
My father is my parachute,
so I keep falling.
my father is my airbag,
so I keep crashing.
My father is the air I breathe—
God knows I've been gasping.

Outside of catastrophic caregiving,
no gravity grounds me to him anymore.
Maybe I am naive, or blind, or plain ungrateful.

God forbid if I'm right,
I wouldn't have words to finish this poem.

Ropar

I am a home to the ones
who are no longer in my life.

Ropar, erected on Harappa's ruins,
is a museum of forgetfulness,
where future glory dims
against its ancient shadows.

I, too, am built on ruins—a tree planted in a cemetery.
My fruits fall, more rotten than ripe.
I bloom but find more autumn
than spring, more ash than seed.

Ropar—my father's city—looks at me like a stranger,
as if we are not mausoleums.

I Am Not My Name

I am a half-written poem,
unfolding through time,
searching for verses in the void.
Obsessed with endings,
I've tried to invent them—
these scars on my wrists,
are failed attempts at completion.

My mother taught me this:
to wage war with life is to become it.
Now I understand why poets bleed.
Each time I laugh mid-war,
I become an olive tree:
roots deeper than graves,
leaves greener than grief.

Call me what you may,
I am not my name.

Hisaab (Hindi)

Hisaab bahut kaccha hai mera!
Mujhe nahin maaloom aankda
Meri toot ke giri hui palkon ka
Aur unpar lada meri
Khwahishon ke bojh ka.

Na main gin paayi hoon apne haath ki lakeeron ko
Jo saal dar saal
Barkat ko mere amal mutabiq
guna aur taqseem karti rehti hain.

Mere qadmom ke nishaan
Darj hain kin kin raahon mein
Aur kitni door tak mahakti hai unki khushboo
Nahi maaloom.
Meri har rag jo dukhti hai uske uthke jaane par
Aur taa'qub ki woh doriyaan
Jinmein main uljhi rehti hoon,
Kise pata kitni hain?

Aakhiri baar jab usne mujhe gale lagaya
Main bhool gayi thi kshan, lamhe, pahar
Aur waqt ko naapne ka
Ratta rattaya har formula.

Anjaan hoon ab tak ke
Kitna shaamil hai ishq mere inquilab mein
Aur kitna manfi hai junoon mere sangharsh se.

Mere ghar ki seedhiyan
Table par rakhi kitaabein
Meri munder par naachti hui baarish ki boondein
Kitni hongi bhala?

Meri bindiyan jo mathe se utarkar
Aayine par chipak jaati hain
Mere gumshuda rubber bands
Mere aawara sajde
Mera mohabbat par fir se
Aur ek baar fir se aitbaar karna
Ganit ki hadon se zara baahar
Ja kar khada ho jaata hai.

Mujhe pata hai gar hisaab kitaab seekh loon
To zindagi kuch aasaan ho bhi sakti hai
Par main toh hoon us rubaiyat jaisi
Jo kisi anhad raag ki dhun par thirakti hai
Waqt ki seemaon ko laanghkar.

Main anant, bebaaq aur behisaab si
Bas udna chahti hoon us pankh ki tarah
Jo pakshi ke tan se toot kar
Bhaari bharkam dharti ki satah par

Kisi halki phulki rehmat ki tarah girta hai
Aur fir udta hai kisi aur hawa ke jhoke se.

Kitni baar?
Kab tak?
Kya pata…
Hisaab bahut kaccha hai mera!

Sunflowers

I take sunflowers seriously.
Rain has my earnest attention.
Some days, my feet sink a little deeper in earth,
and I feel planted—maybe that's why
I talk to trees like they are my siblings,
I borrow sunset colours from the sky,
brew them in my tea,
and drink it like a miracle cure for the diseases
I don't have but carry.

My houseplants will show you the state of my soul.
Ask me about joy, and I will read you a poem.
Hold me in your arms and see how letting go works—or
doesn't.
My lungs have more songs than air in them.
I know grief like I know my hands.
Everything I touch sometimes turn a little sad.
It's a blessing that the moon is out of my reach.

Like love, I'm mostly in the air,
but when I am not, I try to find myself.
I have late-night conversations with Kahlil Gibran,
and I see Vincent and Sylvia laughing in the field my soul
longs for.
Rumi tells me, "You are the field."

But love is ineffable in its expression.
Sara Shagufta's suicide note isn't a biblical verse,
Guru Gobind crossing river Sarsa seems like an act of romance.

So I romance life—and maybe death, too.
I send postcards to faraway places
and write letters I have no address for.
I negate myself often, and then
I negate that negation, and then
I question Marx for the whole process.
He doesn't seem to mind that,
But my comrades do,

I give them answers I don't owe,
judging them as harshly as I judge myself.

Why can't I have faith in the simple fact that I exist?
Sometimes I'm made of noise until a great silence submerges me.
That's where I find God—or a new kind of poem
I become silent even in speech,
like sunsets in their glory,
like rivers in their story,
like I am while taking
the sunflower seriously,
but I am not while writing this poem.

Daarji

I wish I could tell you that after my grandfather crossed a bloody border between India and Pakistan, he lived happily ever after. No. He didn't. I wish I could tell you he became a great man. No, he didn't.

He became a sad man, drown-debris-in-dram man, a micro-manager-of-the-clan man, a young-boy-who-saved-his-life-by-running-and-then-only-ran man, as-if-life-is-a-race man, built-gates-against-grace man, hurt-unhealed-and-gloom man, passed-down-pain-like-an-heirloom man, counted-on-coins-not-cousins man, made-choices-that-broke-his-children man, stuck-to-survival-not-living man, shapeshifted-into-trauma's-wingman, bystander-at-a-backdoor man, died-searching-for-Lahore man, distant-scarred-stubbed man—Oh, he loved us, but never let himself be loved man.

Daughters of Sky

My great-grandmother
sat in a cold cauldron
filled with winter, meditating,
praying to the heavens for a child.
Her husband wanted a son;
she bore him a hurricane—a daughter,
then another and one more.
All her daughters lived long
in places they did not belong,
like a deluge that falls too hard
for too long.

My grandmother
sat in cemeteries more times than I care to count.
She too wanted children,
but lost them all—
some as young as a sigh,
others earlier than decade five.
Some fell from her womb like drizzle,
gone unnoticed in sleep;
others, like sand through the sieve.
One by one,
till there were none.

My mother
sat atop a mountain near hot water springs,
wishing me into existence.
She was a short, bright lightning strike;
nothing was the same before and after her.

I am her first-born.
I think I am rain.
All women of my family—daughters of sky—
probably fell on uninterested mountains,
unwilling terrains.

I have fallen on fertile ground.
My hands are made of will,
my feet of moss.
I think I am going to let my children come to me
whenever they want,
like mulberry trees that sprout up
from childhood giggles,
planted in the garden
and staying long after you are gone,
bearing fruits for generations to come after.

Water under the Flame

Mother had a hack.
Every time, she would light a candle
and place it in the holder.
She'd add a little water to it
so that when the fire burned,
the wax melted and ran down.
It would not stick
but float.

Mother had a hack.
Her rebuke was always watered in love.
Every meltdown of mine
was gently welcomed
by her fluid and flowing affection.

Mother knew: to be bright is to burn,
but that is no excuse
for not soaking your feet in water.

I Was in Several People's Dreams Last Night

I was in several people's dreams last night.
In one, I was painting revolutionary graffiti
on a wall that stood inexplicably in a green field.
This will tell you I come from an era where brushes
and claws were interchangeable. Where art was
the only justice left. Where I spent all my poems
but the grass defeated the concrete in the end.

In another, I was cocooned in the arms of a man
committed to someone else. A man who came
to collect the antidote to his loneliness.
Behind the closed eyes of this toxic ex-lover,
I am guilty of sins I am smart enough to commit
only on the lawless periphery of the human subconscious.
This will tell you I am a witch with a herb garden
of alternative healing. I have birthmarks etched in fire,
but no one believes in magic anymore. In this era,
my cross is not made of wood but of irrelevance.

In another dream, someone took me to a lake
that was off-limits in reality. I even had the skill
of swimming and talking to fish. How do I tell him
I am soluble? Anyway, it's his dream and I have no control.

This means my disabilities can find a loophole
in the constitution of existence. That in the future
I have already learned the art of trespassing and surrender.

In my own dreams, I do not exist.
I am vacating the rented house of my body
one breath at a time.

If that's not introduction enough—
light a candle, say my name thrice,
invite me into your dreams tonight.
I will show you a mirror and in the gospel of self-knowledge,
you will learn all about me.
The futility of this exercise, however,
will dawn upon you in due time.

In Case of Emergency

(after Sarah Kay)

Return my eyes to the front door.
Return my teeth to the knots.
Return my feet to the red bicycle parked in my childhood.
Return my voice to Amy's Song by Switchfoot.

If you find any regrets, return them to the fireflies.
I've always been a hungry ghost for language.
Return all my poems to my grandmother. It was her gift.
Return my smile to the boy I met on the first day of
kindergarten—
The one who made tiny snakes from candy wrappers,
so I wouldn't cry.

If you find anger and mistake it for sadness,
Return it to the first woman my ancestors hurt.
In my books, you'll find pressed flowers of sleepless nights,
bookmarks of strangers who became poems—
return them to the child I was, still learning how to dream.

Return my hunger to 3 a.m.
If you find unopened letters,
return them to the river.
Don't use them to resurrect me.
Return all my postcards to Lahore.

Return my sweaters to my sister, she's always wanted them.
Return unsung songs to my brother, only he can hear them.
Return my diaries to my dad.
Tell him I'm building our next home.
I hope there, I get to grow up in his arms.

Return the leftover food from the fridge to my friends, it's love.
Return my arms to my niece.

There's a grief phone in Michigan,
Strung from a tree trunk.
People go there and speak to those who've gone.
When I am gone, don't go there.
Return my skin to the sky,
Hang my hair like prayer flags,
Return my bones to the man who loves me.
He knows the song to sing over my bones.

REQUIEMS AND LAMENTS

To the One Who Asked Me, 'Shall I Book a Cab for You?'

My heart is as old as uncertainty,
It turns to Vincent Van Gogh's paintings—

Like old birds with broken wings, turn to dancing.
Like autumn leaves descend towards their end.

I have been here before; I'm sure I won't weep, but
rain is pouring on me, and I've got no place to sleep.

Broken People

In a world full of broken people
I once met a boy who
would pick wildflowers
from the fault lines of his past
put them to bed in my books—
or to rest behind my ears.
Either way, they withered away.

Once he got me a pot of Peace Lily,
promising that it won't die on me.
In that moment I knew what hope is;
in the next, I was clueless.

What to do with something that stays?
I left it unattended for days.
What do you do with someone who
refuses to hurt you?
I gave him up like a fumble—a stuttered rhyme
spoken before its time.

Broken people want to love other people;
sometimes they just don't have the skill.
And that's how the world turns into a wreckage,
a little more than it turns into a garden.

Antinome

What if you didn't love me
at all?
Or if I could love you back,
even in pieces—
we wouldn't negate each other like that,
like an inevitable tragedy
in the queue,
a grenade's pin coming off.

You were consistent
in your pelting,
and I was relentless
in my resistance.
But what if when you loved me,
I could love you too?
Then we'd dance together
on the West Coast,
like Bombay Showers
and Pacific waves
making love.

In Which I Confess and Curse

I feel some of us are essential to each other's journey. As if we need a partnership beyond romance and attachment. Like we would never become who we are supposed to become without coming in contact with one another. We need them and they need us. Lovers.

Then, some of us are designed to operate alone. Even the slightest proximity to another's attention, embrace, or love dissolves us into molecules, scattering us across space. Sometimes it takes a lifetime to build ourselves back, and even if by some miracle we are able to do that, every broken and strung-together part of our existence fears any kind of intimacy. Loners.

It's crazy how some souls work in pairs and in units and other souls just cannot. But it is crazier that there are also souls like mine. The third kind.

We are made up of leftover soul parts of lovers and loners. We long for and repel love at the same moment. So we suffer. Our bodies are made of constant conflict. Our hands are made of disharmony and our skin is coloured with distortion. We carry the scent of conversations we never had.

We are lotuses in a muddy pond—our beauty inspires metaphors, evokes awe. But we cannot bloom outside the muck, so we cling to it. Our whole life becomes an act of finding ourselves.

We must love and lose, love and lose, love and lose—until even loss loses count. They say that God is close to the brokenhearted and so we bless him every time we are wrecked. We see God's face when we are shattered. We are his grand, glorious fuck-up—and oh, let us adore him!

Even for this. Even in this. Still—praise, praise, praise!

Agar Magar (Hindi)

Meri har baat ka jawab
Woh 'Agar Magar' mein deta tha!
Main likhti thi use
Apni naadaan chaahatein
Bebaak sapne
Hadon ko paar karne ki
Koi chunauti
Aur woh tajurbe ke taraazu mein toalkar
Honi anhoni ki chhaanni
Se chhaantkar
Rakh deta tha mere saamne apne
Agar aur Magar
Main har baar unhein uthakar
Phir likh deti thi
Ek nayi umeed ki nazm
Woh har baar use bina padhe
Aage badh jaata tha

Is This What Dying Feels Like?

I haven't heard my voice in a few weeks.
No one has called my name.
No one has touched me—seen me,
a silhouette strolling the halls of absence,
no witness, no words.
If no one is loving me,
do I even exist?

Held Captive

in my long-standing gazes
these days, the ceiling fan
makes a lot of noise. It jitters
like dismantling itself into freedom.

Perhaps it'll smash my head into oblivion,
or mercifully crash into the window
                                    sideways,
perhaps it'll fly away like a spaceship
looking for roots
                elsewhere.

How much anger must I have for myself
to believe that everything will either break me
or forsake me?

Even on the sacred island of my imagination,
I seem to have abandoned myself.

Dil Kya Hai (Hindi)

Andhere ki ik siyah chaadar
Jis par dararon ki
Meenakari hai.
Dard ki rahasyamayi
Guththi koi
Khud suljhne mein hi
Guzari hai.
Baaz log
Zindagi ka markaz bhi hue,
Mujhe ab un
Markazon se bezari hai.
Mohabbat mili aur
Haathon se fisal bhi gayi,
Kismat pe jaise
Afsurdagi ki pahredari hai.
Shadeed dard se shuru
Aur ik aah par khatam,
Darmiyan kuch nahi,
Zakhmon ki teemardari hai.
Munh ke bal girna
Aur phir sar uthana,
Safar marzi ka nahi,
Hausle ki karzdari hai.

In Which I Ask for Towels

Towels are more useful than husbands
who cannot love you.

If only I had something left in me
to write a poem about towels.

A hot bath could have cured me
if I had any skin left.
I am beyond wanting now,
not even water will do.

It's all pain now, and even
that's melting away.
words don't set me free anymore.

I've found a new art—
one I shall do exceptionally well.
No, not poetry. Death.*

I promise it will stay on your lips
longer than any of my poems,

As for my sweat, blood, and tears,
ask for the towels.

---

* This phrase is borrowed from Sylvia Plath: Dying / Is an art, like everything else / I do it exceptionally well.

Broken Antenna

Sun spills over my roof.
I search for the traces of you.
My fingertips are burnt
from combing the gold
for any sign of you—
grief is no map,
love no lighthouse.
My longing a broken antenna,
and you—a voice in the void.

The Descent

On certain nights, the moon descends,
burdened by my grief. Rubber plant
bows its head. Even my cat turns away.

Sorrow spreads its tendrils,
colonizing the land where desire once lived.

Listen: even crickets abandon
their songs to my laments.

After the Flood

In some houses, beds float
like private islands.
Here, I sleep on a paper boat.

I rise with every sorrowful tide—
my body, a fragile craft
bobbing in sadness.

Perpetually sodden, perpetually drying,
bearing the watermarks
of every storm weathered,
every flood survived.

Yaani (Hindi)[*]

Hua nahi ishq uske baad yaani
Ab talak ho barbaad yaani

Uske dil se be-dakhli ke baad
Nahi raha koi makan yaani

Apne hafize pe rashk tha tumko
Ab aata nahi yaad khud ka naam yaani

Dhoond rahe ho almaari mein dupatta uska
Chhota pad gaya aasman yaani

Ik aah tak na nikli haaye
Badi zalim thi daastaan yaani

Kitni siyaah nazmein kaafi hongi
Kaise karoge qissa tamaam yaani

Aane bahaane karte ho uska zikr
Aati nahi jaan mein jaan yaani

Itna hanste ho kyun hanste ho
Bhool gaye ho muskaan yaani

---

[*] Co-authored with Amir Malik during a baitbazi session.

Saari duniya ke ilzaam use dekar
Rafu karte ho apna girebaan yaani

Ab gulmohar nahi lagte aur peele phool
Saari galliyan hain sunsaan yaani

Bilal mar gaye maine masjid se tauba ki
Phir di hi nahi kisi ne azaan yaani

Rishte bante hain toot jaate hain
Ishq chadhta nahi parwan yaani

Use tumhare har waade pe aitbaar tha
Tum nikle faramosh be-imaan yaani

Mohabbat ki sadaqat ka bharam hi rakh lete
Usme bhi rahe badguman yaani

The Body Keeps a Score

How to explain
the way skin holds history?
I recoiled—
not from his touch, but from the ghost
of yours, still etched into my flesh.

The past fondles me through the present,
between his fingers
and my skin, I carry you.

In this the treacherous landscape
of my hedgehog body—
His touch does not erase; it only overlays.

Kal Shaam (Hindi)

Jab tumne apni mehboob ko baahon mein lekar
Apne kamre ke darichon ko
Chaand ke muhn par bheench diya tha,
Tab wo chaand
Mere ghar ki chhat par
Pehli baarish ke ruke hue paani mein aakar doob gaya.

Maine badi mushkil se
Use apni hatheliyon mein bhar kar bacha liya,
Apne saath munder par bitha liya.
Aur phir, meri jaan?

Phir humne saari raat baithkar
Tumhari jheel-si un aankhon ke baare mein baat ki
Jinmein kabhi hum doobkar
Jee sakte the, mar sakte the!

Drowning

It's alright, this fracture in the boat.
It's allowed, this moment when wholeness splinters.

Some nights, the only truth
is the acceptance of rupture,
the embrace of what cannot be mended.

Does it matter now—
who tied the weights?
Who chose the water?
The descent continues.

Grief, like the sea,
knows no bottom.
Arms refuse to breach the surface;
legs have forgotten how to tread.

This drowning—
may it be the last.

PROTEST POP

Aftermath

Eight years after June 1984*
I was born to a mother
pregnant with the tragedy of losing her brother in the
aftermath.
Trauma runs through my veins.
It runs through the households of Panjab like
exposed sewer lines—
it stinks,
it breeds death.
Our old family albums
have pictures of branches
gone missing from the family tree—
some as young as ten springs,
some as old as ninety.
Our women—upright and strong,
bent and broken by the vigilante
and the forces all the same.
But who is to blame?
So a daughter invoked Waris Shah
to the grief of Heers of Riverland;
our mounting pain could rise
and eclipse forever the sun,
our screams could summon

---

* The Indian Army's military operation at the Golden Temple, Amritsar.
The operation led to significant civilian casualties and anti-Sikh violence.

God on earth, for justice

But justice or closure
has become like the second coming of avatars.

I hope—and as I hope, I fight.
Resistance is my second nature.
Love, my freedom song.

I, an offspring of an aftermath,
cannot forget 1984
without forgetting to exist at all.

Shehar (Panjabi)

Chandigarh 'ch bahar vele vi
Patjhad vaangu phull digde ne
Concrete dian sunniyan imartan 'ch
Jaan pai jandi hai
Sadkan kisse peer di dargah vaangu
Rangeen chaadar heth dhakiyaan jandiyan ne
Main sochdi aa onhaa loka baare
Jo ae shehar usaaran khaatir
Ethon ujaade gaye
Oh pind jiss de pinjar
Saadiyan neenhan heth madhole gaye
Main vekhdi aa kiven
Jadon ukhaadhe dakhatan nu
Sajde karde ne
Is shehar de firdosi phull
Har mausam ethon da kiven
Khushi 'ch vi thoda udaas hi rehnda hai

Barish (Hindi)

mere shehar mein
ek ajeeb si barish hoti rehti hai
aasmaan se ladkiyon ki
tasweerein girti hain
ek boodhi amma rehti hai yahaan jo
paagalon ki tarah sadkon par
daudti rehti hai
un tasweeron ko ikattha karti hai
chipkati rehti hai
kabhi kisi deewaar par
darakht par
bus stand ke bench par
aur kehti rehti hai
meri beti lautaa do
meri beti lautaa do

kaunsi beti
kitni betiyan

mere shehar ke
chand fikarmand log
chalk se footpath par likhte hain
'justice'
justice for kathua, unnao

bastar, assam, delhi, kolkata*
kaunsa shehar
kaunsa kasba
kaunsi basti
kaunsa ghar

jahaan nahi mili ik ladki ki laash

jab mere shehar ke
saare log so jaate hain
woh tasweeron wali ladkiyan
aapas mein baatein karne lagti hain
kehne lagti hain
hum to kahin nahi gaye
hum to yahin hain
apne aas-paas dekho
ek aur ladki laapata
hone ki kaagar par hai
use to bacha lo
aur woh naam leti hain un ladkiyon ke
jo gumnaami mein maari gayin
jinke chehre ko koi

---

* Kathua (2018 rape and murder of an eight-year-old in Jammu), Unnao (2017 rape case and suspicious death of survivor's father), Bastar (ongoing conflict zone and human rights violations), Assam (systematic rapes by army personnel in militarized zones), Delhi (2012 Nirbhaya gang-rape that sparked nationwide protests against sexual violence), and Kolkata (2024 rape and murder of a junior doctor highlighting violence against medical professionals).

tasveer bhi naseeb nahi hui
jinke liye kisi ne protest nahi kiya
jinke liye kisi ne kavita nahi likhi
jinki awaaz koi nahi sun pata
siwaaye us boodhi amma ke

aur mere shehar ke log to suna hai
masroof hain
us azaadi ke jashn ko manane mein
jiske parcham hamari reed ki haddi mein garhe hain
par kal jab akhbaar ki sukhriyon mein
ek aur ladki ki tasveer chhapi hogi
tab aap kya karenge?

rape jokes par hans denge
ya ik nai fehrist nikaalenge ki
humein zinda rehne ke liye
kya-kya karna padega
ya phir apne ghar ki casual misogyny ko andekha kar denge
ya phir humein takleef dene walon ko parliament ki ticket
de denge
ya kuch dareendoon ko jail se parole
ya phir se kahenge ki
is mulk mein to ladkiyan deviyan hain
koi mandir banwa denge
aur aasman se ladkiyon ki tasweerein yunhi girti rahengi
ek boodhiya hai paagal
woh kehti rahegi

meri beti lautaa do
meri beti lautaa do

aap kya karenge?

Yeh Kavita Ek Elaan Hai (Hindi)

Yeh kavita ek elaan hai—
Hamari aankhon ke khwaab
Hamare dil ki namrata
Hamare zehen ki bebakii
Hamare ishq ki barkat
firkaaparasti ki
Bheint nahi chadhegi!

Ham har subah uthenge
Bhagat Singh ke khaton ko padhkar
Aur aazaadi ko apna maqsad bana lenge
Mohabbat ko apna markaz bana lenge

Ham jaga lenge
Tumhari jhooth ki lori mein doobkar
Soye huye zameeron ko

Ham Faiz gaakar tod denge wo fansoon
Jismein awaam ko tumne zakad rakha hai

Ham awaaz dekar wapis bula lenge
Un apno ko jinko
Vikas ka jhansa dekar
Tumne azaab mein dhakel diya

Ham protest karna sikha denge
Un parivaarjanon ko
Jo apni soojh-boojh ki keemat par
Tumhari Whatsapp University
Mein daakhil ho gaye

Tumhare mazhabi bantwaron ke vidroh mein
Ham Mardane ki rabaab par
Guru Nanak ko gaayenge

agyaanata ke andhkaar ko
Fatima aur Savitri*
Ke pratirodh ki lau se bujhaenge

Tum taanashaah ho saheb
Zulm tumhara amal hai
Ham lovers, lunatics, poets
Haqparasti ka farz nibhaenge

Safdar† ke nukkad natak ko
tumhari gali le aayenge

---

* Savitribai Phule and Fatima Sheikh: nineteenth-century educational reformers who established India's first school for girls in Pune, 1848.
† Safdar Hashmi was a playwright and street theatre activist, killed while performing a workers' rights play in Jhandapur. His death became a symbol of artistic resistance and cultural activism in India.

Tum nafrat ko hawa doge
Ham aman ke nagme gaayenge
Tumhare diye har zakhm par
Jazbe ka marham lagaayenge

Bus to aap jalate hain
Ham Manusmriti jalayenge*
Naqab bhi aap pehente hai
Ham sare aam sare maqtal aayenge

Aur baat yeh bhi sun lijiye
"Ham kaagaz nahi dikhayenge"

Tum jab jab jabar ki laathi liye
Hamari jaanib aaoge
Phir kisi deewane ko samvidhan uthaye
Jaama Masjid ki seedi par khada paoge

Shaheen Bagh ki auraton ke dam se
Sadaf† ko jail mein bhi azaad paoge

Mehnatkash logon ke haathon se
Faasiwaad ki qabr khudwaoge

---

* Manusmriti Dahan (1927): Dr Ambedkar's public burning of *Manusmriti* at Mahad Satyagraha, marking symbolic resistance against the caste system codified in the ancient text.
† Activist and teacher arrested during anti-CAA protests in Lucknow (2019), became symbolic of state action against peaceful demonstrators.

Hitler ki chaal chloge, saheb
To Hitler ki maat hi khaoge

Kyunki abhi to Sabika* ke kajal se likhe
Inquilab ki subah hona baaki hai
Abhi to Amir† ka zindagi par phir se
Ikhtiyar aana baaki hai

Abhi hamare seene mein dhadakti aag baaki hai
Tumhare saare zulmon ka saara hisaab baaki hai
Secular India ka sunehra khwaab baaki hai
Abhi to ishq baaki hai abhi inquilab baaki hai

---

* My friend, poet, editor, educator known for progressive poetry and grassroot activism.
† My friend, poet, and journalist during the CAA NRC protests wrote to me that: *jaise zindagi par ikhtiyaar nahi raha (it seems I've lost authority over my life).*

Hathkadiyan (Hindi)

(2 January 2018)

Unki ki hathkadiyan Ahed* ko
Jakadne ke liye nahi bani

Wo hazaaro saal purane
Pratirodh aur sangharsh ko
Jakadna chahti hain
Jiski muthi banakar
Ahed ne unke
Pet mein ghoonse jade hain

---

* Ahed Tamimi: Palestinian activist from Nabi Salih, known for her resistance since childhood. First detained at the age of sixteen (2017–18) after confronting Israeli soldiers, she became a symbol of youth protest in occupied territories.

Agar Ab Bhi Chup Rahe (Hindi)

Agar ab bhi chup rahe to
Phir kab bologe?
Bohat si aankhein sawal karti hain
Bohat se haath madad ki guhaar lagate hain
Agar ab bhi chup rahe to
Phir kab bologe?

Ramjas college mein protest pe baithi hui ladkiyon ke baal
kheeche jaate hain
Haath unke kapdon par nahi
Unke wajood par daale jaate hain
hostels ke bahar bikes pe sawaar Bharat Mata ke thekedar
Jaaykaare lagate hue unhe
Balatkaar ki dhamkiyan dete hain
Kahte hain—aao baahar ... le lo azaadi
Tab unki dari hui, aakroshit aankhein
Humpar aa girti hain aur puchhti hain
Agar ab bhi nahi bologe to phir kab bologe?

Bohat se ladko ko uthaya gaya
Bekaar samaan ki tarah
Police ki gaadi mein daal kar
Thaane le jaakar ek kone mein phenka gaya
Phir un par laathiyon ke saath saath
Desh drohi hone ke ilzaam bhi barse

Aaj unke badan pe pade hue nishan
Aur un nishanon ka laal neela rang
Hamare safed ho chuke lahoo se puch ta hai
Agar ab bhi nahi bologe to phir kab bologe?

Hamari maa ne hamara maatha choom kar
Humein vidyalaya bheja tha
Kaha tha jao,
Wo mandir hai!
'Vidya vichari to par upkaari'
Aur aaj hamare vidyalaya
shamshan ghaaton mein tabdeel ho rahe hain
Kahin Rohit* ke haath se kalam chheen kar faansi ka
phanda thama diya jaata hai
To kahin Najeeb† ko hostel ke kamre se uthaa liya jaata hai
Eent eent girte hamare vishwavidyalaya ki deewarein
hamara darwaza khatkhataati hui puchhti hain
Agar ab bhi nahi bologe to phir kab bologe?

Pata hai…
Bhagat Singh ki awaaz aur hamari awaaz mein sirf ek hi fark hai
Unki awaaz behre kaanon mein bhi goonjti thi

---

* Rohith Vemula (1989–2016) was a Dalit PhD scholar in Social Sciences at the University of Hyderabad whose death by suicide, on 17 January 2016, became a watershed moment in India's discourse on caste discrimination in higher education.
† Najeeb Ahmed was a student at Jawaharlal Nehru University (JNU) who has been missing since October 2016.

Aur hamari hamare andar hi dafan hai
Ham band kamron ke andar
Mahfooz baithe hue
TV ki chhoti si screen par saara tamasha dekhte hue
Yeh prarthna kyun karte hain?
Ki koi krantikari phir se laut aaye?
Kyunki humein hamari apni awaaz khokhli aur bemani lagti hai
Lagti hai, par hai nahi.
Agar hoti, to zara socho
Ek seminar
Ek samvaad
Ek nazm
Ek Gurmehar*
Hukumranon ko yun khaufzada kyun karti?
Agar aaj main tumse kahun ki tumhari
Ya meri khud ki
Aur Bhagat Singh ki awaaz mein koi fark nahi hai
phir tum ab bhi nahi bolo ge to phir kab bologe?
Yeh awaaz hamare gale se nahi nikalti
Jise ghot kar koi chup karwa lega
Yeh awaaz to kranti ke us garbh se nikalti hai
Jo sar katne ke baad bhi goonjti rahegi

---

* Gurmehar Kaur's resistance (2017) marked a significant moment in Indian student activism, initiated through her 'Save DU' campaign at Delhi University. Her protest began with a social media post holding a placard that read 'I am not afraid of ABVP', following violent clashes at Ramjas College.

Isliye maine apni aawaaz ko apna hathiyaar
Aur apne dupatte ko apna parcham bana liya hai

Aur abki baar jab wo
Aankhein chadhaaye
Aur haath badhaaye
Hamari or aayenge
To ham darenge nahi
Ham unki aankhon mein aankhein daal kar kahenge:
Tumhare dene ki hoti to tumse maang kar le lete
Par yeh to hamari hi hai
Aur ham lekar rahenge
Azaadi

Sar-e-aam (Hindi)

Dekho! Sareaam humein aazmaane lage hain,
Ab zaalim goliyaan chalaane lage hain.*

Purzor bahere kaanon mein jo goonj rahi hai,
Isliye humari aawaz dabaane lage hain.

Bevajeh to nahin qase hain shikanje apne,
Imam, Aazad, Gogoi unhein daraane lage hain.†

Auraton ke jin geeton se pareshan hain woh,
Unhe gaane mein humein zamaane lage hain.

Khanjar, goli, laathi, jail sab aazma lo,
Hum sadko se uth kar nahin jaane lage hain.

Shikasta pa mat samjho hausle hamare,
Hum aandhiyon mein chiraag jalane lage hain.

Zahir hai ki dara hua hai ahl-e-haqam,
Maloom hai takhton taj dagmagaane lage hain.

---

* https://indianexpress.com/article/india/shaheen-bagh-firing-caa-protest-6246745/
† Activists detained under various charges amidst 2019–20 protests. Sharjeel Imam (JNU), Chandrashekhar Azad (Bhim Army), and Akhil Gogoi (Assam) faced extended imprisonment for their role in civil rights movements and anti-CAA demonstrations.

Naakaar (Hindi)

Phir kahin
Ek phool khilega,
Phir uske saamne
Saari
Tabaahi
Naakaar saabit hogi.

Letter to Lahore: Are You Cold Too?*

Dear Lahore,

How are you? Is the wind too cold there? It is here, so I am asking. And no … it's not winter. We both know it's not! It's the ice of people's hearts in my chest. The poison we are consuming in a futile desire to kill the enemy. Only that we do not recognize the enemy. Misunderstood history is the enemy. Spoon-fed hatred is the enemy. No, Lahore, you are not my enemy.

So I am asking … Lahore, are you cold? Not because of me, but because of the hearts beating inside your chest. Your wind has begun to cover my windows in mist, and I am wondering… have your people started to consume the poison too? Can't you recognize, Lahore, I am not your enemy.

Recently, a shop named Lahore Chowk was changed to Lucknow Chowk, and I was shaken. The cold winds are blowing from each side. The fire is dancing in our eyes. The ice is settling in our hearts. We are both inhaling poison, wishing to blow death on each other's face. Or to plant the kiss of betrayal on each other's lips. Who will go first?

---

* The first letter I wrote and sent to GPO Lahore in 2016.

Lahore, our lungs will soon cease to function. And all the inhaled poison is going to make graves in our stomachs. Shouldn't even the thought of it cripple us both? Why can't we still recognize the enemy?

Poison is the enemy. Cynicism is the enemy. I am not your enemy, and you are not mine. We are both victims here. Now I am shivering, giving in to the cold. So I am asking … Lahore, are you cold too?

They say love comes naturally to the human heart, and hatred is taught. So I am asking, can we unlearn the hate? I have also heard that moving closer makes us warm, and warmth kills the cold. I know you are shivering too … So I am asking … Lahore, May I hold you? Can you pull me closer?

It is cold, but it doesn't have to be.

Pyaare Lahore (Panjabi)

Tere vehre de meen 'ch bhijje
phullan varge dost jadon watni parte
taan unhaan ne mainu teriyan
bohat gallan sunaayiyan.
Tere burj tere bazaar
tere boohe tere birkh
tera moh tera pyaar
tera maan teri jhirk
teri har shai da tarjuma
unha apne haasyaan naal kita.
Lahore, main saara kujh
chupp chaap sun di rahi
fer main apne hathan val vekhia,
khaure kehre janam
ishq ne tera naam
mere hathi likhia.
Khaure kyu mukaddar
us te leekan vaaiyan?
Teri taangh 'ch uthiyaa
mera har kadam,
meriyan reejhan
birha di choli paaaiyan.
Fer vi har waar
meriyan akhaan ne
begaaniya nazraan naal

tera deedaar kita.
Lahore! Main bahut tutti
fer tutt ke
tainu pyaar kita!
Teri mitti nu matthe laaun vaali
tere naan te nazman lutaun vaali.

Letter to Lahore: Friendship Day

Dear Lahore,

How are you? I've been thinking a lot lately. My bookshelf grows more 'anti-national' by the day. Amrita, Sara, Guevara, Rumi, Neruda, Brecht, Faiz, Gibran, and Pash have become my roommates. They sing freedom songs and whisper love lullabies. Their magic must be rubbing off on me – how else could I find the courage to write you this letter?

Our borders, with their divisive nature, remain meeting points – altars of burnt offerings and friendship candles. I've burned even my heart for you. It's been nineteen years since our countries went to war. Is hatred in remission? Are we friends now?

When I make tea in the shade of your sunset, Lahore, I wonder: are you blushing at my hopeless romanticism? Do you drink the peach of my skies too? In my dreams, I stroll your streets, peeking into houses where people watch Hum TV. Would you dismiss me as a stalker or take me home tonight?

I wonder, is your telephone network also clogged with forwarded messages on the first Sunday of August? This can't be lost in transition or translation.

Lahore, you must find my words floating on the wind.
Return them with a kiss. Or more ... I don't know how to be
your enemy. I only know the pain where my limb once was.

Happy Friendship Day.

Your own heart beating gently in Chandigarh,

Amy

Letter to Lahore: Daak

Dear Lahore, how are you? Let's travel in time, shall we? I was fourteen years old, half tucked in a small bed next to my mother's in a huge hospital in Amritsar. Trying to tune in to radio stations to keep me company, When I first stumbled upon your fearless, seditious radiowaves.

Main hairaan thi aur behad khush bhi ki in tarangon ko nahi rok paayi Wagha Attari ki koi sarhad. Mujhe yakeen tha iske baad gar mujhe jeena hai to kuch is tarah awaara, bebak, bekhauf jeena hai.

After that, every night your radio sang songs of my heart! I went to bed with City FM 89 singing me to sleep! I'm twenty-six now. This morning I woke up to Lahore radio paying tribute to Mehdi Hassan. So I quickly took out a postcard from my collection and wrote:

'*Kis kis ko batayenge judai ka sabab hum, Tu mujhse khafa hai to zamaane ke liye aa*'*

Sent it to: General Post Office, GPO Chowk, Shahrahe-e-Quaid-e-Azam, near Anarkali, Mall Road, Lahore 540 00. I have posted it on my way here and I wonder what will happen when it reaches you. Lahore, will you write back to me?

---

* From Ahmad Faraz's ghazal 'Ranjish Hi Sahi'.

Dekho na main sarhadon ko saraab kar aayi hoon, Faraz ne kaha tha so dosti ka haath badha aayi hoon.*

Lahore, will you hold it? A friend called and said, 'Amy, we're going to Lahore with a play in July! Can we bring something for you?' I said, 'Can you bring Lahore itself?' He laughed, so I said, actually, I do need a few things:

Thodi mitti Jilani Park ki jise main roz Garden ki har kiyari mein chhidka dena chahti hoon.

Thoda paani Ravi ka jise Satluj mein milaakar Panjab ko uske kho chuke maayne lautana chahti hoon.

Kaan laga kar sun na wahan, Bhagat Singh, Rajguru, Sukhdev ke Inquilab ke naaron ki goonj hai, main use apne gale mein samaa lena chahti hoon.

Ik gaon hai mere daarji ka jahan main kabhi nahi gayi, wahan ke kisi buzurg ke haathon ka saaya main apne sar par oadha lena chahti hoon.

Noor Jahan ki ghazlein, kuch ansune lok geet jo shaam hote hi jawaan ho jaate hain. Unhe apni zubaan par sajaa laana main unhe gungunana chahti hoon!

---

* Ahmad Faraz's sher: *Agar tumhari ana hi ka hai sawaal to phir / Chalo main haath badhaata hoon dosti ke liye*

Suna hai "Andaroon-e-Lahore ki baaz galiyan itni tang hain ke agar ek taraf se aurat aa rahi ho aur doosri jaanib se mard to darmiyan mein sirf nikah ki gunjaish bachti hai."

Main us gunjaish ko bhi aazmaana chahti hoon!

And there ... as I was about to say more, he interrupted me saying, 'I understand, Amy. I'll bring Lahore itself. I'll have to bring Lahore itself!' So tell me, Lahore, will you come? I will keep the door open. I will lay the table with homemade aloo parathas. Will you come and dine with me?

Kyunki edharle Panjab da saara kuch te odhrele Panjab da saara kuch mainu haale vi apni daadi de sandook 'ch paye onha dariyan, bistaryan wargaa lagda jis te bachiyan di poori malikiyat hundi ae.

So tell me, Lahore, apni jaydaad ka lutf uthaa lein? Saari lakeeren jo haayel hai darmiyan unhein mita lein? Attari ki lohe se bani unchi sakht deewaaron mein hum dono kuch masoom bolti khidkiyan bana lein?

In hope of the day when this letter will no longer need an international postal stamp.

Chandigarh to Lahore wali,

Amy

Soft Rock and Serenades

Tonight

(after *Agha Shahid Ali*)

Mad heart: what troubles you? Why do you ache tonight?
Looking for your mother again, what's at stake tonight?

My home made of phantom pain, walls full of dead frames,
I could've stayed here, but stayed for whose sake tonight?

Life-giving hands that made Santiago wrestle and win,
Wrote: 'The sun also sets.' My heart will break tonight.[*]

Ibn-e-Mariyam's[†] hands bought my salvation, hallelujah!
May I now kiss Judas? May I bless his mistake tonight?

Amy, the divider of the Red Sea, is not blind to you,
If he brought you here, please, wait by the lake tonight![‡]

---

[*] A nod to Hemingway's *The Old Man and the Sea* and his suicide.
[†] Jesus Christ (Son of Mary in Islamic tradition)
[‡] Evoking the biblical story of God parting the Red Sea for Moses to deliver the Israelites from oppression.

Note to Self

Dawn approaches. Radio plays on.
No one in the world knows he's gone.
In this cocoon of sweet delusion,
you are still in love—stay there.
In these infinite final moments
where loving him no longer requires his presence,
even when the song is over,
even when home turns into ruins and rust,
even when you are the only person left
to carry love in your chest—
love, still.

Love Thy Enemy

i will not spend
my good mind
hating you.
will not give you
that much room
in this house
of my thoughts.
instead i choose
this cleaning out,
this clearing away.
whatever pain
had your name on it
gone now
like smoke
through a window.

Faustian Bargain

Newspaper headlines—
I have sent them on a cold trail.
I don't let hatred and war
slip through my door.

I don't order panic attacks for bed tea;
I don't buy heartbreak in everyday EMIs.

The world continues to burn,
but I have a room. Somewhere to bloom.

I have given up my sight for my sanity.

Too Many

When too many years have passed,
It's possible to forget the day your mother died—
a sublime presence of memory
fading against the sandpaper of time.

When too many years have passed,
it's possible to misplace your divorce papers,
watching grief turn
into just another obituary.

When too many years have passed,
it is possible to lose count of fractures.
But La Loba remembers what we forget—
how to make an animal from bones.

When too many years have passed,
too many years have passed
for it to hurt
anymore.

Tweezer

Death is not a grim reaper
appearing in the dead of night,
harvesting lives in one quick swoosh—
a single moment, defining and definitive.
It is a tweezer.

It comes for the air first;
second, it takes the warmth.
Memories, which are many,
are its most tiresome task.

This tweezer starts with the
worst memory
and takes it away.
That's why all people appear good
once they are dead.

As I write this,
another memory is being pulled out
from behind my ear—
was it my mother's kiss?

Memories are slippery,
quick, stealthy,
and great hiders—

death's biggest enemy,

They are time travellers;
They can hide in photos and diaries,
also in songs and poetry,
sometimes in a recipe—
you saw your mother cooking when you were eight,
but will remember only when you are eighty.

And it will then conjure your loved one
back into existence.
Fleeting as it may be,
it defeats death.

Death at its zenith is amnesia.
Memory, even at its weakest,
a déjà vu,
a seed breaking
into rebirth.

A Wall

Sadness is a wall
between you and me.
My ode stands between
the mango tree and me.

Every time I write to you,
I reduce love to its description.
Each poem I read aloud
is stolen from my silence.

All windows are a separation.
Each adjective, a cage.

Today, I want to erase every word I ever wrote.
Yet, I'm writing this poem—
more words about my dislike of words.

Do you see now?
Words stand between you and me.
I really want to talk to you—so much so
I can't stand the subtle atrocities of:
expression,
language,
labels.

Love is a form of silence.
Poets, a goddamn noise.

Camouflage

Some women hide
behind men—fathers, brothers, sons,
lovers and husbands.

They think of themselves as creepers,
never trees.

Some women hide
inside books, written and unwritten,
escaping things unspeakable—
living life a dream's width apart.
They like to know how the story ends.

Some women hide
in their work,
high-functioning anxiety,
only good for a bank balance
and social capital, but
never for a good night's sleep.

I was once a woman hiding under her own bed.
Now, I spend all my days
pulling her out of there.

This Too Is a Prayer

I wish you pain;
not the kind that cleaves hearts,
not the fatal blow.

Instead:
forgetfulness, when you seek old graves;
loneliness, mirror to your fractures;
fatigue, when rage seeks revenge;
a splinter in your heel, if you want to hurt;
a cramp in your leg if you walk away from love—
small reminders of the language
you taught but never spoke.

I wish you pain:
painful enough to make you human.

Vessel

When I wailed,
my city shattered
like glass.

Yet the ocean
Remained unmoved.

Pain etched poetry in sand;
waves edited with each caress.

Fear learned to dance with peace.
I poured all my noise into the sea;

In its depth, I found only silence.

Shards of Truth

Moments scattered in glass
like a shattered vase—
what am I to do with these pieces?

I could catch moonlight in my garden,
sprinkle glitter on my dupatta,
make kaleidoscopes of memory.

In each shard, a different face
looks back at me. Which one
tells the truth?

Perhaps truth itself
is what happens after
the breaking.

Arrival

I think about the first person
who wrote a poem.
What moved their heart?
How did they know what to call it?

Poetry comes to me sometimes
as a translation of a forgotten language,
as a squeal in my throat,
as an opening in my dam heart.

It arrives like a letter just in time—
as jasmines bloom
and my lover is home.

Poetry comes as an answer,
sometimes as a question,
sometimes a test I cannot pass,
sometimes as a breath of fresh air
after staying underwater for long.

Kavita Da Safar (Panjabi)

1
Pehli kavita nu
Naaz hai
Ki oh pehli hai
Us vich beej ne
Pungaran di chaah hai
Pehli kavita suchi hai
Pehli kavita saaf hai
Bebak hai

2
Doosri kavita
Chalaak hai
Us nu pehli kavita ton
Wadda te add disan
Di parwah hai
Doosri kavita
Pehli kavita di
Ikklauti jodi daar hai
Saani hai
Doosri kavita aazaadi hai
Manmaani hai

3
Teesri kavita ne
Pehliyan kavitavaan

Ton sikh ke
Apna navaa raah
Banaaya hai
Teesri kavita beparwah hai
Baagi hai
Teesri kavita kalam kalli
Teesri kavita vairagi hai

4
Chauthi kavita
Jaani pehchaanee
Aam jihee
Jis di kise nu udeek nahin
Jis di kise nu chaah nahin

Jo likhi gayi
Kyunki kavita taan
Likhi jaani chaahidi hai
Kyunki kavita taan
Sab likh rahe ne

5
Panjvii kavita satt hai
Zakhm te aaya khareend hai
Khurpi da vaar hai
Apni andarli kise doonghi
Teh ch utaran da asar hai
Panjvii kavita sudhaar hai
Jaan sudharan lai tiyaar hai

6
Chhevi kavita
Sarhad parli waaj hai
Eh kavi nu pichhe laundi
Bada bhajaaundi
Door lai jandi
Kise maidan vich
Jitthe kavita da vavrola hai
Par kavi nu us di bhukh nahin
Sago'n Kavi nu us ton ohla hai

7
Satvii kavita
Chupp hai shaant hai
Adol hai
Satvii kavita bei (nadi) ch
Utarde guru da vismaad hai
Satvii kavita anhad te anaad hai
Dhadkan ch thirkdi
Loon loon ch lishkdi
Satvii kavita boli hai
Eh nira noor hai
Satvii kavita is duniya ton
Bahut door hai

8
Athvii kavita
Kadi likhi nahin gayi
Likhi nahin ja sakdi

9
Nauvii kavita
Bahut vishaal hai
Buddh waang jagdi hai
Maai bhaago waang maghdi hai
Heer waang gaayi jandi hai
Rehndi duniya tak sunayi jandi hai
Nauvii kavita har zabaan
Da pehrawa pehn
Kull dharti te vichh jandi hai
Nauvii kavita baani ban ke
Kudrat vich ris jandi hai
Nauvii kavita navii hai
Pehli kavita waang hi
Darasal
Nauvii kavita
Kar ke hi kavi ton
Likhwaai jandi hai
Pehli kavita

10
Dasvii kavita
Likhi ja rahi hai
Likhi jaayegi jad
Ho jaayega kavi
Apni kavita ch vileen

Mad Woman

No one likes a mad woman.
Mad woman has submission amnesia—
she can laugh off false promises,
save herself some time, some pain.

Mad woman has a bitter tongue;
she no longer dips it in caramel.
Only her whims and fancies are sweet.

Mad woman has come into her anger.
She is red. She is blood.
She screams. She is flames.
She doesn't hold back her words,
for they keep her held back.

Mad woman is hysterical.
The world taught her to cry, be shy,
but she laughs like thunder,
or popcorn from a broken machine—
sadness marinated in sunny flavors.
Mad woman jumps from roof to roof,
dream to dream, sometimes man to man,
womb to tomb, after her heart.

Mad woman is free.
No one likes a free woman.

Mahila Munch

Once a month,
we gather—
women with thick thighs,
in high heels,
sisters with fat arms
and big waists,
in the middle of deodar trees,
near silver rivers and moonlit peaks.
We, the women, gather to eat.

Ripe mangoes and bitter gourds.
Cheesecake and jasmine flowers.
Roghni naan and mint chutney.
Sourdough bread and rajma chawal.
Our spread is lavish,
and flavors are many.
We have caffeine and wine,
water and whiskey.

We light the fires
in the shape of sacred spirals,
place many pots and pans.
We cook, we dance,
we swim, we sing—
all night long we eat,

more than we want,
more than we need.

I am the soup maker.
I take leftovers and boil 'em
into elixirs of rest.
We dine in solidarity,
for our pleasure alone.
We break bread in the names of
our sisters who are gone.
We bite into the night,
until stars spill into light,
and no one is left wanting more.

Cheesecake

Never eat cheesecake at the museum's cafeteria—
it's like setting yourself up for disappointment:
committing the mundane to memory, tinder lust to
matrimony.
Chances are it will be stale, a half-told tale.
Don't you find it strange? There's no room for exchange
here in history's showcase. It's not a birthplace
for a baker's delight or a romantic hindsight.
Never look for love at the museum's cafeteria.

In Which I Rescue Beauty

I bought nails;
I will *hit* them with a hammer.
Each hit will thrust one
into the wall—damaging
craters to create space for art.
Then I will *hang* it
As if I have to *punish* it
for existing in this world.

Why is the language of adding beauty to home so violent?
And what is it about *capturing* and *framing*, and
caging something in wood, metal, or glass beautiful anyway?
Why does Beauty make *executioners* out of us?

Perhaps my hands
could learn to open, not to own
to witness, not to wall
until beauty walks freely

through rooms I thought needed stolen aesthetics
leaving no scars,
no holes,
nothing imprisoned,
nothing owned,
just a living touch

that stays because
it's free.

Calvary

You can't cross half-hinged, half-fallen bridges.
You can't scoop the lava in your bare hands.

You can sit with me under Orion
and talk about your dead cat.
You can bring your coffee mugs stained
with her lipstick and use my dishwasher.
I go to church every Sunday to see how
it has forgotten to take Jesus down from the cross.
That's how I cope with the nails in my hands.

You can sit with me under the steeple.
and watch me confess the sins that aren't mine.
But you must not claim me as your saviour—needing me
to hang from the cross, bleed out, go to hell and return
on the third day. For you. The last time I returned, I
brought a little piece of hell back with me.

I will not offer my body for the blows meant for yours.
I will not shoulder your cross. You are welcome to
knock at my door and I will draw a map for you.

But it is a long walk to Calvary. And it's *your* walk.

Autumn's Hope

The rains have retreated, leaving me
at the threshold of autumn.
What to do with my heart,
this fragile, feathered thing?

I offer it up: a song
of remembered storms,
and scarlet hope.

Somewhere,
apples ripen in silence.
Light changes its mind.
Leaves forget how to hold on.
The sun, once fierce, grows tender.

Perhaps this season
will show me mercy.
Perhaps I will learn
to be kind to myself.

Khud Farebi (Hindi)

Kuch baaton par
Woh ahmaqaana gussa
Apni jagah,
Ki jis mein tumne
Mujhe chot pahunchayi,
Mere dil ko toda.

Par gae roz,
Jab apni ne'maton ka
Aanchaal tatola,
To dekha ki tumse
Mila bhi bohot kuch hai.

Aur woh sab jo tum
Mujhe nahi de sake,
Use tumse paane ki talab
Mehaz khudfarebi thi,
Mere dost,
Mere raqeeb.

Mujhe maaf karna,
Apni hasraton ka ilzaam
Maine tumhare sar rakha.

Aur is khudgarzi ke liye,

Khud ko maaf karne mein
Mujhe kaafi der lagi.

Are You Still in Love with Me?

Night falls.
The world leaves us.

In this room, I stand—
shedding guard, façade, bandage.
Naked, I let you see me.

You, who admired me from afar,
tell me: are your hands
made of sandpaper or balm?
Are you strong enough to be gentle?

This mosaic of fractures
that drew you closer—
see how it changes in this light?
Can you love what darkness reveals?

I offer no promises, ask for none.
Only this: be the period
at the end of my sentence.

Balm

I promise
the night can't scare you
anymore than you have been haunted
in broad daylight.

When the times are dark,
times are blessed too—
like the world that rests
at the back of our eyelids,
half situated in the colour black.

Your darkness has a home;
call it and make it your own.
The night has the balm
for what was burnt in the day.

One Thing

If we knew the language of our hearts we would have known
this already but it took a virus to shake us up to the truth—
We are all one thing. Everyone affects everyone.
My well-being is linked to yours. Your pain hurts me too.

When the supermarkets all close, I'll need to borrow
from you what I lack. I'll fill your cup from my bottle
when it runs dry. We'll be one in quarantines.
One in each other's arms. Filling groceries in the kitchens
of daily-wage workers.

Drawing constellations of 'inquilab' when the roads are left
empty.
Feeding moonlight to the stars lit dimly on the hospital
beds.
Giving the extinguished ones back to the skies in the boats
made of reverence and grief.

We'll kneel in awe of our masked warriors who took
suffering
and turned it into compassion. Foraging new paths between
do or die.
Building lifelines between die or die.
We'll speak life through our tongues and build a world
like writing poetry—crafty, aesthetic, eco-friendly and free.

Our hands shall rescue other hands from the washbasins of capitalism.
Invoking love that sings from the rooftops and balconies.

Yes, I would draw a line between us because I love you enough
to love you from a distance. From across the glass windows of isolation wards and Skype chats.

And I know that on the other end of this terrifyingly beautiful journey
you will erase all lines, defy all borders, dub every boundary
a convention to meet me. Like the sun that sinks into the sea –
gently and at once. Like they were always one thing.

Two Pigeons

—homebodies and co-tenants in quarantine
live in my *roshandaan*;

they are lovers—or perhaps it is just spring—
but they often wake me up
with loud lovemaking.

At first, the kisses look like bickering;
aggressive pecks soon subside into affection,
to the patient eyes, arousal reveals itself.
Instead of moaning, they flutter their wings loudly,
sometimes abruptly as if caught midstep,
in their romantic waltz.
To the sound of my broken Turkish,
they dance like no one is watching,

Yet I watch them, and I fear:
Death has been to my house frequently—
its eerie silence is a mist on my memory
I recognize its scent so much so
I can now smell it from miles apart;
It leaves my house emptier, heart heavier.

Lately, life too has started speaking to me—
an omen here, an *ishara* there

This morning, I found
bird eggs nestled in a clay pot in the balcony.
Life making room amidst gloom.
How do I respond to mercy like this?

Hoş geldiniz, haytam!
(Welcome, life!)
I'll be fluent in the here and now.

Surma (Panjabi)

Jadon main akhan 'ch surma pauna chhadiyan taan
Sab nu main bimaar jihee laggi
Jo vi milda—puchda
Tuun theek hain?
Shaayad hi kise sochiya ke
Suhapan de duniyaavi maapdandan ton pare
Kiven lagdiyan ne ikk kudi dian akhan?
Kise da mann parchaoan ton baahar ki hunda hai
'Theek' hon da matlab?
Hor kis shay lai thaan hai meri akhan 'ch?
Par kise nu safai den
Te sawaal karan de bojh ton baahar
Main apne aap nu bahut sohani laggi
Te 'Main khush haan' keh ke
Agge vadh gayi.

What Should I Call You?

The first vertical fine line on my forehead.

Skyscraper. Stonehenge. Exclamation mark. One half of
holy cross. Call a doctor sign.
Thin line. Tall order. A river. A border. A stick. A trick of
old father time.
Now that you are here—now that you are mine—
what's your name?
I don't have retinol on me;
I am wary of sunscreens too.
I don't want to expel you, just tell you: Welcome!

I never thought I'd have the privilege
to arrive at the threshold of old age.

Salvage

These days I'm hooked on the idea
of salvaging my heart.
I am recovering its shards from
the underside of the doormats
of people I have loved.
I have opened an online relief campaign—
I let strangers be nice to me.
Somebody wrote to me: 'Neferes'—
word for beauty in ancient Egyptian.
Hayder Ergulen's poems have become
my 'Nafas'—word for breath in Turkish.
I am breathing from my belly again.
I am hollowing my heart
to the point of such softness
it can no longer break.

To-do List of Love

- Plant flowers in my hair.
- Phone me when it's raining.
- Make hugs an integral ingredient to the recipes we cook in our kitchen.
- Don't call it spring unless you've smelled it on my back.
- Let the trees bear mangoes now that they have seen us kissing.
- Make moonlight our bath bombs.
- Make stars a road-map of our communion.
- Let no sunset skip our windowsill.
- Let no song go without slow dancing.
- Don't let the night fall before falling into my arms.
- Make my smile the sun you say morning prayers to.
- When the world comes to a standstill, let me meditate on the sound of your heartbeat and tell me my world hasn't ended.

Two Tunes

Two moments have gone by. Two tunes played.
A song in the making—life's become
a lullaby on the creator's lips

I feel like a freedom song
in the making—far from it, yet
I sound like longing,
like hoping,
like breaking in parts
and coming together,
as jazz tunes
jamming into perfect
harmony of night.

Naghma (Hindi)

Chanda dareeche mein
Aankhein meeche main
Baithi hoon gum sum
Si yahaaan

Aake tu chhu le to
Khud me piro le to
Ramm jaun tujhme
Main zara

Shaane pe
sar ko rakh ke
Gayein naghme
Kya rakha hai jag me
Tere siva…

Teri saanso ki hararatein
Karti hain jo bhi shararatein
Kaise ban jaati hain chahte
umr bhar ki raahatein

Jhilmil sitaron ki
Chadar chinaaro ki
Ghere hain
Apna aashiyaan

Pal pal ki malmal ye
Jharna sa kal kal ye
Behta rahe
Darmiyan

In the Language of Trees

You water dead plants,
as if grief were a kind of hope.
I collect newspapers from the porch,
stories of a world we don't inhabit.

At the breakfast table,
your eyes search for the door to yesterday.
I offer words like bread,
knowing you won't eat.

Noon finds me among your books,
on pages you once touched.
You stand at the window,
mapless at the atlas of loss.

When birds return to their nests,
you ask what home means.
I point to the bills on the table,
our names side by side.

You drink coffee as if it were medicine
against remembering.
I set the table, you set the alarm.
We both know sleep is a fickle god.

On the roof, under stars,
I spread a blanket over the scars
of your sky.
You sit. You look up.

I try to tell you:
You are not a flower,
to be plucked by the hand of this season.

You are a forest, evergreen,
roots deeper than my knowing.
But my words are pebbles
in the vast sea of your silence.

So I sit with you in the dark,
learning the language of trees:
to stand, to weather, to grow
in spite of the axe.

In time, you may remember:
even the oldest forests
were once seeds,
breaking open in the dark.

Love, Like Laundry

In the hum of spin cycles
I feel it—love's turbulence.

Isn't it always this way:
taking what's soiled,
steeping it in forgiveness,
until the water runs clear

The fabric of us emerges,
altered, yet familiar,
its creases a map
of where we've been.

We hang our hearts to dry,
press out the wrinkles
with gentle heat.
And then,
we wear it
like belonging.

What Is, Is

I should have left a heart a heart and a stone a stone.
I should not have turned a song into a door,
or a door into a prayer.
I should have left a border—a border, a scar, a scar.
I should not have turned it into a stitch or a river.
I should have known better than to turn
time into a compass pointing everywhere but here.

Longing was longing, until I shaped it
into ladders leaning against an empty sky.
I should have let the clock remain a clock—
not a requiem playing by the hour.
Time was always time, until I made it
into a fishnet cast for things water doesn't return.
Memory was memory until I wore it
like a perfume that rubs off on other people's skin.

In love, I have personified objects.
In desire, I have objectified people.
In truth, I should have let it be.

Ghar (Panjabi)

Ikk tutte hoye ghar di aulaad hon de naate
Main lammi umar ikk ghar di talaash vich rahi
Darakhtaan diyan uchiyan mazboot taahaniyan
Abba dian unhan baanhwaan wargiyan lagdiyan
Jinnah vich simat jaana hi
Salaamati da saboot hunda

Jadon vi kise nadi de kinare chali taan
Us de sarot takk pahuchna chahiya
Jivein koi bachha maa de garbh
Vich mud jaana chahunda hai
Ghar da naksha talaashan

Kade main panchi hoyi jo sunia si sirf
Tinkian nu jod ke bana lainde ne ghar
Kade-kade mainu kise da dil vi
Lagda si apna basera
Jithon kadhay jaan da khauf hi
Mainu utthe jaan nahi dinda si
Mohabbat di ghalatfehmi vich
Kai hatthan ton zakhm khade
Je jism rooh da makaan hunda hai
Taan bass dheh jaan ton theek pehlan
Bacha liya si main apne aap nu

Kise diyan akhaan kade-kade darwaza
Lagdiyan taan

Main unhan 'te dastak dindi
Par bahut saare darwazey
Sirf biaaban vich khulde
Main fer be-ghar hi reh jandi
Phir kavitaavan likhan lag payi
Te kiraaye de makanaan vaang
Unhan nu badldi rahi
Jadon kite vi reh na saki taan
Sochiya apna ghar banaundi haan
Zindagi di taqseem vich
Kuch pungaran di gunjaish si
Main maali ban gayi
Har daraar ton ikk daastaan uggan lagi
Har khidki ton ikk sufna
Khindhe aalhneyan de pankheru
Aun jan lagge
Tan ehsaas hoya
Hor ghar ki hunda?
Kise da ho jaana
Kise nu apna laina
Mitti naal mitti hundiyan
Guldaudi uga laina
Dupahir sarkay
Pyaar chaaven beh laina
Jhuldiyan haneriyan nu
Sabr naal seh laina
Apne kalaave nu ena vadda kar laina
ki tuhade saavein koi beghar na rahe

Answered Prayers

Sarah's* God was listening
to their mockery of her barren womb,
to her silent tears in the night.

Millenniums later,
at the ending of our story,
you said to me:

'You will never be loved.'
'You will never be whole.'

Then hurled your curse:

'You, Barren Woman!'

My God was in the room.
He was listening.

---

* Sarah was the wife of Abraham in the Bible who remained childless into her old age, enduring mockery and shame until God fulfilled His promise and she bore Isaac at age ninety. Her story symbolizes both the pain of infertility and the power of divine intervention.

Plato Said Poets Are Liars—Then Why Do They Live Forever?

When John Denver's plane crashed, songs fell like rain from the sky. Every radio in every house became a harvest tank for that rainwater. California became a hymn, sung for forty days straight. Pilgrims on country roads finally reached home.

When they came for Lorca in Grenada, his body absorbed all the iron this world refused to bend into pens—iron that was forged into bullets. Spain wept for its patron poet of unholy prayers. They never found his body, but if they had, they would have uncovered olives in his pocket and a ticket to Cordova.

When they came for Pash in Panjab, it was because he said, 'The most dangerous thing is for our dreams to die.' Dream killers pried open his body with guns, searching for the vaccine of his verses. But he hid them elsewhere. You'll find them in Barnala—where a jungle of green grass sings his name.

When Forough's jeep collided in Tehran, her poems flew through the broken windshield. Some said they became parrots, others swore they turned into crows. All agreed, though, that those feathered things could sing from the deep end of the night—of the deep night ending.

When Parveen Shakir's car crashed in Pakistan, this dame of desires—this azad nazm—rose like attar from a shattered bottle. Young girls soaked her fragrance in their hair. We learned to turn to her poems before we turn to our lovers. Even now—can you smell her on me? On you?

Agha Shahid Ali grew up in a country without a post office, yet he knew the world was full of paper. "Write to me," he said. Against God's vintage loneliness, he wrote a chant. On the Day of Judgment, I bet they'll say, "His mad heart was the bravest of them all."

All his life, Mahmoud Darwish was planting beautiful flowers in cemeteries. He didn't know who sold his motherland, but with every poem, he took stock of who paid the price. He watered rivers that died of thirst. He turned into rain and stone and everything—then nothing—in Houston, not Palestine.

What indifferent governments can do to a state, indifferent husbands can do to a wife. When Sylvia Plath turned on the gas, every oven in London learned to speak in pentameter. They recited the story of Lady Lazarus. Here she lies—alive, furious, eternal.

When Amrita Pritam took her last breath in Delhi, every train to the afterlife stopped. Waris Shah stepped onto the platform to receive her. Young girls wrote her poetry on their palms with henna. She will meet us again, she promised. *Main Tenu Phir Milangi.* Have we not fashioned our lashes into welcome mats?

One night, Surjit Patar went to sleep, opened a door, and joined an eternal chorus. I can still hear him singing through that door. Long before that night, he told us he wouldn't be here forever, but his songs would remain— like a separation pressed close against the heart. Will our children not sing his songs?

And just now, in Gaza, they bombed Refaat Alareer's home. Kites loosened up in the sky. His last testament: a poem— 'If I must die, you must live.' So here I am, a poet. Your poet. Breathing, writing, holding on to what others cannot. Is this the truth? Is this a lie?

I don't know who lives forever, but poets—we do not die. Plato.

Acknowledgements

Pehla shukar Parmatma nu.

With gratitude, I remember Dr Surjit Patar—the one who believed in me, my expression, my voice, and inspired me to be brave and claim my space in this world. Wherever you are, this is because of you.

Preeti Gill and Shantanu Ray Chaudhuri: thank you for your faith in my voice and for bringing this book into being. For the candles you light on my path, I am forever grateful.

Niyati Singh, thank you for wrapping my poems in your painting. I'll let people judge this book by its cover because it's perfect. Thank you for the harmony, thank you for colours.

Rochelle D'Silva and Meghna Prakash: my friends, fellow poets, and first readers/editors of these poems. You told me my poetry has a place in this world. Without your encouragement, my imposter syndrome would have silenced this book before it began.

Meneka Shivdasani, your mentorship, though brief, transformed how I approach craft. Thank you.

Nirupama Dutt and Neelam Mansingh: you have inspired me in more ways than I can count. Over the years, I have learned by watching you both practice your art with courage and brilliance. Thank you for trailblazing and opening doors for my generation.

My family on earth—Papa, Roop, Manpreet, Rajdeep, Neyamat, Alambir, and Mamiji. My beloved Snoopy and Ocean. Thank you for your love and endless grace. I dream because of you. I am strong because of you.

Ma and my family in heaven—thank you for watching over me, for being my eternal support system. I feel your presence, your quiet strength, lifting me from above.

My friends—Ashima Chugh, Amir Malik, Anu Verma, Daisy Mann, Harish Mahla, Jassi Sangha, Kanupriya, Manjot Khangura, Monam Arora, Pallavi Singla, Sabika Abbas Naqvi, Sawan, Sonia Chauhan, Soumya Joshi, Sukhdeep Sukh, Vijaya Singh, and Zubin Mehta—across years, timelines, and continents, you continue to illuminate not just my poetry but my life. Thank you for being my witnesses, my guardians, my secret keepers, my healers, and my kin.

And Nik, my love—thank you for loving me so purely and ardently that I feel like I can do anything. This book, and this girl, are anchored by you. This is a small offering next to all that you do for me. I love you for singing over my bones.